T0114879

After Three

SHANETTE PULLUM

authorHOUSE®

AuthorHouse™
1663 Liberty Drive
Bloomington, IN 47403
www.authorhouse.com
Phone: 833-262-8899

Published by AuthorHouse 02/24/2021

ISBN: 978-1-6655-1789-8 (sc)
ISBN: 978-1-6655-1790-4 (e)

Library of Congress Control Number: 2021903685

Print information available on the last page.

Introduction

After Three contains poems of many different kinds to usher you through a journey of the writer's heart, her knowledge, and her love for writing. She has put together a book consisting of childhood love to present to you.

Poetry is one of the best medicines. She believes it can lift you up from your state of sadness, or it can sadden you, but either way it allows you to experience another's journey. This will help you to understand that so many around us are going through a phase of love or an unkind moment. There are so many things that you will know—about untold moments, or the feeling of just sitting and enjoying nature.

The author encourages you to shine, whether your moments revolve around the heat or the cold. The beauty is not staying where life has hit, but to pursue the better—be inspired by these poems as you internalize them.

All Is Not Gone

When the terrifying earth gets warm,

Corruption pools itself to the top of life

And creates live streams borders,

All is not gone.

When disease rides the earth,

Like it is its chamber.

When fire consumes our earthly treasure

And volcano renews,

Like it was welcomed to elope in earth's beauty,

All is not gone.

When our dreams grow thorns

Making it impossible to hang onto,

And our heads cannot station

Among the living,

All is not gone.

We have the power to wail,

Hate the moment of earth on its axis,

But allow ourselves to live—

For all is not gone.

The Bruised Tree

The bruised tree might lose its roots.

It might lose its arms,

Even surrounding warmth.

The bruised tree can die

Under the red sun,

But there will not be a line of complaint

From its injured stump—

Not from its head,

Neither its bed.

The bruised tree will stand

Firmly in the sand.

It will fight in silence.

It will cry on course from its pores,

But will perform all chores.

The bruised tree has the strength

Not to be sickened in time of trouble,

But to grow from inflicted wounds,

Without grave sounds.

A Place

There is a place where the river grows dark.

Where trees bundle and bark,

And where the line of the mountain

Appears thick like a loaf of bread.

It is where the sun seems to be unseen.

A little trod of humane feet were just not the team.

In the cold of secret dark,

It was too long a journey to the moon.

If you just go the distance

Of the part of earth that seems so dead,

You would be so engulfed as you rise to the star.

The Running Children

Woman and men, look at the running children!

Aren't they your petals from a fine plant?

Where are you to return them to the branch?

Their existence should not be wild,

So let them reattach to their roots.

Don't let spring, summer, autumn, and winter

See the tremor of their bodies,

Parading with lack of hope,

And clutching to wasted spills.

As shoppers delay from their fright

To balance the unfair world,

Create a new atmosphere for attraction,

And give them the functional root.

Did I Love You Enough?

Did I love you enough

When your hands failed from toil,

The edges of your toes boiled,

And the roses of your cheeks

Could not withstand the pain?

When weakness emerged in the darkness?

Did I love you enough

When you did not realize

The opening and closing of the sun?

When your feet could not reach the ground

And you could hardly hear a sound,

Did I stay to be your chaperone?

Did my shadow bring you comfort?

In your dream of dreams,

Did my feet come forth in a team?

In the sphere of the new moon,

From the tears of your lame body,

Did I love you enough?

The Heaviest Heart

The heaviest pain lives

Upon a heart that is not free.

It curses your cheek

And lessens your meek.

It blocks your imagination of greatness,

And stifles your feet.

The heaviest heart permits no fun.

It interrupts safe sleep,

And hangs your lungs steep.

It paves no way for love.

It keeps its path closed

While your soul will browse.

You Didn't Come

You didn't come to fetch me,

And my feet bore the pain of loss.

Upon my heart, it could be a better way

In the wideness of the day.

I made allowance for your late words.

I may lose my head at this minute,

For this is a horrible moment.

I will continue to dream and not lament.

The beginning of my loss

Is here with hope to hold.

Your untouched hands,

I know it will bond.

Dad, can't you see you are still my heart.

I cannot change it and I will not try.

Turn around for I am behind,

Waiting for my dad to find.

Discover Me

Discover me when I am not full of life,

And when my cheeks shrink

From the absence of mild.

Devote your love in my cry.

Take my wheels and help me to steer

From my grown and half-empty pride,

And my non-polished side.

With your outstretched arms,

Let me see the reason to be strong,

For we are one.

If you could go back to history and many songs,

Nothing is gone.

The backbone is alive; the skeleton provides;

Rise to the call of your ribs.

The Strength of the Moment

Enjoy the moment of the moment,

That you see a world filled

With broken and unbroken things.

You have the power to change,

Or not to change;

With your intellect you will breathe.

If you shall lose,

Have the nerve to cheer every moment of life—

Losing is the face of experience.

Rise from this course of installation,

Don't distance yourself at the bottom.

Enjoy your moment; live through the falling things.

Don't

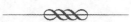

Don't judge me by the harvest of another,

Nor the curved and rich life of my brother.

Don't judge me by the texture of my skin,

Nor anything that comes from within.

Look upon me with your mood,

But remember to remain smooth.

Don't inscribe the face of another,

In your steam of unbalance for your brother.

The Disturbance

Knees downward in the wide space;

Heads with different thoughts stretched for a mile,

As the magnet of the sun made full penetration.

Who knows each pain!

There were different women,

Braving the weather,

Toiling to mend their homes.

Her eyes pulped from her station in the bushes.

Many days the fade of the blue bird's song

Gave her a chance to center her eyes on their labor.

The glittering sun just could not win,

For their arms were swift, like banners flowing in the wind.

Seriousness echoed from the heart of the field

That seemed dried from hours of patience.

The scream caused much grief,

For it seemed to set all apart,

And the field was void.

She didn't know she could play upon the settled minds.

She did, and regretted,

Although the bee was to be blamed.

The Light

Her heart raced like a confused stream.

With eyes fixed in the sky,

The pain wilted in the air.

Her feelings hanged in the hot cigarette

That lifted her spirit like an eagle.

The velvet path was now erased,

Like an old drunken man,

Crashed the harder miles

To look back at the unlighted,

As war penetrated the sky.

The Dead Crowd

The smell of fresh coffee stood

In the midst of the crowd of the surviving voices.

The air shoveled in thick attires,

With long soft tears shining.

They tried to find out the mystery,

But the fresh air propelled more tears,

And less answers for a cherished love

That was too deep-rooted to close.

For hours they hugged the final resting place,

Which was carved by skilled hands.

His home brought satisfaction,

But not to the unending tears

That spiraled in the air,

As his pleasant journey returned

To the arms of mother earth.

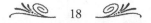

Gone Is the Music

Gone is the music with its passionate form.

From the center of this night,

A message of injustice lies.

A weeping heart to face a leisurely wake,

A grief to follow with no clarity,

Also a world to greet with no future,

For his animated smiles were erased from the sunset hills.

The full day will not be better—

Not with his silence.

No Smoke on the Hill

There is no burning—not today.

The world is quiet.

I paused, but I was not crossed,

For there was no sleeping van

To carry a soul to lie.

My wide mouth kissed the clear air.

Only the long, winding stone lingered of old,

Upon the breast of the wind.

The crying of heads in the still evening

Was the climax of happy hearts.

His Heart

We were pinned on the log,

Waiting for his arrival.

It was the perfect hour,

When the sun fell behind the clouds.

We looked forward in hope,

Through our blood for the changing moment.

That is why today his half-empty hands have torn us apart.

We knew he wanted to change the world

Just for our sake.

Seeing him so close to falling,

We could only first stretch out in hugs

To give him the urge.

He is not alone; not with our lights.

Granddad

Granddad, I wish you would wait

Until I build a hill of memory of you.

You chose to go just too soon—

A little before I could anchor that spoon.

I was inspired from your run.

Your dormant tears were never seen,

For you never seem to reverse from your toil.

Oh grandpa, I hate those boils.

They landed on your feet

When the shoes did not sit well to the miles

That led to the market site.

For hours you went in the blazing sun,

Bearing printed sweat on your brows,

With not even a sign of frown.

You came home at the budding of sunset,

Sometimes with the same weight,

And the love to repack.

There were added duties to lessen

With the heavy sun that was charged,

But you would shout praise,

Despite your long traipse.

Granddad I wish your life could restart.

I feel so disoriented.

Forever you are gone.

Your focus and strength

Would kill slavishly,

For sometimes things feel like hell,

And I know you would make it well.

You're My Mother

Life had separated us on many occasions.

Those long hours at school—

Mom to tell you the truth,

All of my heart was not there.

I am overwhelmed for a little in my ears,

And it advanced each and every day.

It was so baffling, mom, to be away,

Within the gate of the schools.

The books had me crying.

Missing you made my story poured.

The tears bled and the wounds nursed,

With the nearness of your far away heart.

From a Child's Heart

My dad, I wondered what you would do.

When I was a child,

If I fell and hurt my knees,

Would you pick me up neat

As I struggled to meet?

Mom did it with drops of tears,

But I know it was because she felt strained.

In the afternoon, why were you not there

To divide the toil,

Showing me love with mom

With a bedtime delight

To soften my life?

Mom did it with drops of tears,

But I know it was because she felt strained.

Would you teach me many great things,

Like how to ride a bike,

Or how to hike?

Mom wanted to, but she needed the support

From an amazing heart,

Not available in her path.

The Emptiness

Uncle Jack had requested we stay.

Our hearts, like a touch of light,

Shimmered from his blue cloud of smiles.

We have not seen him for ages.

He wasn't a part of the extended valley,

Marching around with his declining years.

We counseled him on his shortcomings—

That appeared to revive his face.

On our route, the pain of beauty ravaged.

The loss of youthful walls,

And the souls of many, left him breathless.

He grew cold from his missing steps.

We cheered him along

From the remnants of our souls,

For we knew he was dying

From the aches of yesterday.

We hope he will pardon

His pervading scorches, then move on,

As he breathes upon what was good in his years.

The Windy Night

In the night, the drained wind

And the moaning of the outside trees

Took the beaming evening,

And abandoned the completeness of my thoughts.

Your face was lively like the earth's bee,

Though the dead wall cried

From the patch of light.

So scared was the little faith that lodged

Inside my partially dead heart.

Yet your firm in-route created a newer me,

As I witnessed soft face

In the heavy unpredictable forecast.

It was my clearance in the darker world.

This Earth

Oh beautiful earth,

Made by voice;

And the full sea creatures,

Named by wisdom.

From far and close,

Flowers wild and cultivated,

In the shining sphere,

Formed the death of the night

And the beauty of the day.

Oh, Mother

Oh, Mother Earth,

You place focus on the trees,

The animals, and man.

The glowing sun bonds

With startled beauty,

Hugging as you sweat through.

Old World

Old world, there are so many things

That can manufacture tears.

You camped upon my soft bed.

I could not fathom the scene

Of your fortitude.

Old world, life is not strong.

It is thin like the thinnest of thread.

Like a ripe fruit that magnifies age,

The active wind may take a portion,

As it competes with the sun to tear along.

Old world, your bolt face is here,

But I will not allow it to nail me

With the roof of confusion,

Neither complication in this path.

I will not take—for my side is the better.

Richness

Money is like a prisoner

When health has no sitting on wise earth,

And is presumed to be stored,

To rust, and supply nothing.

The results of great wealth

Should leach to the naked souls,

The deep ugliness of unused land,

The awkwardness of animals,

And the expounded injustice of mere men.

The Ongoing Journey

I braved through the sun.

This night I stared back at the profound days,

And I gave praise, for I have me.

I shared my guilt

From my innocence,

As I settled in the mirth of summer.

I triumphed, like a child

With the last dark, then usual dreams.

The sun opened for another chapter

In the mass of the heat.

It may rain—but I have to walk,

And create my dream.

The Other Side of Life

When the unresolved tongues

Of humans go flying,

Never let it clothe you,

Nor crunch your head.

Live in your beauty,

Not in the unpleasantness of earth,

Nor the route of tears.

Life has twists and turns.

You will always be you,

And only you should fill your path.

Supply it with your pursuit dreams,

And the fullness of laughter.

The Sounds

If you should think about sleep,

Don't listen to the sounds at night.

Uncounted sounds sprinkle rudely

Behind the windows and doors.

The airplanes with their midnight sobs;

Nudges on the lazy roof.

With the twining air you watch

That rising twig through sunlit maze.

Don't listen to the last of its remains.

The breathless songs of birds fill the space.

The big buzzing mosquitoes,

In their band, grow fat with the dark.

If you should think about sleep,

Don't listen to the sounds at night.

The Blinded River

I have seen the sleeping river

In the midst of the panoply of the forest.

Its humorous life seems to die

From the choking pieces of branches.

The bouncing trees with greenery

Make the hurdles of the river seem difficult.

It spoke so loudly, like my dear life

Had no zest to ride the dark shore,

To move freely upon earth.

I stood, with my immature vision,

Where no fruit lay.

I wish this dear river will pass this station,

In the midst of the utterance of rain

That may remind of its strength,

So I may pass the tears

Of the ugliness of what life brought.

Night Falls

When night falls, sleep—sleep!

The day has gone.

Don't bring the roaring trouble

Into the freedom of your space.

The sea is there;

The wriggling ponds stay afloat;

The mountains remain.

Leave them, with the freedom of the outside,

In the solitary mist.

Don't sponge in the pain,

Not on your side.

Roll them out

In the chances of the tide.

When you see the tree dancing—dance.

When you see the sun shining—shine.

Walk safely with the ugly—

Backward, not forward.

Sit upon earth with sentiments,

And create a new page.

From Inside

We are equal.

We are all the mixture,

From one man and one woman.

Who dares to challenge!

It may be otherwise.

From my head, there was no choice—

Only in the wise garden.

Don't let the nature of your hair,

The confusion of your tone,

The flame of your fame,

Suspend equality from your soul.

The high mountain can fall,

The greenery of plants can grow weak,

The dashing river can fail,

And we can die without being dead.

Don't let hate cut someone's walk.

Safety Bounded

The strange flower tangles

When its eyes get pressure from the sun's play,

And the grazing animals

Breathe downward in sight.

The sturdy creature will dwindle

On the ageless earth.

The passion and pursuits of the glittering things,

From man's heart will never be green, not forever.

All in its depth will wane in the dark,

For earth downward will die.

Safety is bounded up high.

Colder Temperature

A half man in the twilight,

His sorry soul revealed

The many lost evenings as they sprouted.

In the rock he should find wisdom

For the answer to the question.

In a deeper journey is now the crust

Of the mortality of his heart.

Write Me

Write me a poem of your thoughts,

Plain and simple—

No rhythmic drills, dashes, and tilts.

Put yourself in,

And everything within.

Bright and deep from your gut,

Lose the noon.

Give me the day when the sun is wise.

Let me reach your bright eyes under the sky.

Write me a poem—a poem!

That does not lack beat.

A poem for meat.

A spontaneous poem that is true;

A poem I can feel the gravity through.

The Lonely World

Gone from my room, a fine breeze,

And my heart squeezed,

For a head failed in the clouds.

From earthly length and crowd,

A mist of cold white, I'm not proud.

Gone like the ocean tides

Is the smile so wide.

Like sulky smoke uploaded without wise,

In its falling hour,

Eyes wept for the beauty of a flower.

Little Children's Smiles

Don't tear away childhood's songs,

Neither childhood's plans.

Don't weaken little children's smiles;

Don't cut their future miles.

What will happen in the future

When they later mature,

For you keep coming at their feet,

Sinking them without a chance to meet.

It is not fair for a fallen plant.

Don't spring the hard tears.

Let us understand,

And not create a loveless land.

His Hour

The flower had sunken from sweetness,

And the reducing power

Had left him in the dark.

His heart climbed to many repeated lines

Of a kingly hour.

There was nothing much he could do,

But wait heavenward for an answer

To bring him to the shore, then he would curl.

The depth of the sea had imprisoned him,

For he forgot he should be a deciding factor,

With the speed of the tide that hurled.

Wise Words

Live upon the wise words

Of the fuller hearts,

That aged by the sun's grace.

Upstairs experiences and manners compact

From permitted toils.

Reward, bruise, and closeness,

With nature and religion.

Teary Heart

The insertion of a teary night,

Motioned his eyes to the fractured note.

The privacy now—none,

As the crowded ocean took the journey

To the forefront.

The flowing imperfect world,

The burning scars like the aloft engine,

And the secret heart poured aloud.

He could not clutch the noise

That disbursed from the rapid furnace.

Tonight his heart shall not be stone.

The clouds will shred alone.

The moon will not sing—not in his close space.

Like flapping birds, he will fly.

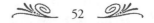

Leaves from My Hands

Flowers cut, left the edges of crumpled leaves,

In the palm of my fist,

From the seclusion of my garden.

The judging of multiple details,

Smoked the spiral pain in my heart.

The insertion of dance,

Marries the bloom with the sun

That popped among the morning plants.

It swept the past from the mist of my face.

The Old House

An ancient house, that measures the distance

Between me and my inflamed heart,

Is hidden in the wild.

It broke a smoke of smile,

Each time my steps rest,

On its sour sides.

It dashed in the river of the past,

Slowly, as I breathe.

Children from my growth

Were not allowed to stop at this beauty.

Our dreams in the street could only be printed

On the sidewalk edges.

The Trench

I saw him in the scaling square.

Cutting through with strong hands,

Measuring in the fighting minutes,

His dreams upon the rock

That summoned his feet.

His lashes hanged high,

Swarming from the tears of the sky,

As he held to his drive

For a clear journey with his hands.

The Old Car

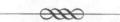

An old car resigned at the back—

Beside the old kitchen tent.

We think pass its wheels of no dent,

As we drive this car with our knees.

In the cool thriving breeze

When the silver rain showers,

We watch the awkward bunch of flowers,

Right beside the bend,

That kept our shade then.

Our whole hearts were new,

And for a few hours

We claim it ours,

Until our mothers call from noon.

The Coconut Tree

There is a coconut tree

That sweeps yonder sky.

It hikes my head to see its fruits

From my side.

It is crazy high for my eyes.

Yet I like to observe it when it fights

With the speedy crushing wind.

Not to break apart the immature nuts,

For it will drain tears.

That Is Not Enough

That is not enough

Is the cry of the man who knows;

There is just some more success

To embrace in a warmer earth.

That is not enough,

Cried a man with strength,

And wants to fight—

Fight to move the stagnant dark.

That is not enough,

Said the man who has eyes,

To see from low—

To the greener mountain unseen.

That is not enough,

Said the man, who hates to lie,

From where he is affixed.

He knows it is not his truth.

They Paid the Price

From their unseen tears,

They gathered every morn,

With shouts from their heads,

For a better side.

They set their blue and red backs,

As the sun battled with the spirit of arms

That ached from a future of nothing.

In their long deep journey.

Some rethink their times

In the dull nights.

Their soreness brought plans,

Among stronger minds, of freedom.

Watching the line of their faithful blood brutalized

From higher hands, their bodies took the beat in their entrance.

They could not nap, not with the opened door,

For they murmured words of freedom.

The Barren Field

Looking at the long wide journey,

Her tempo rose in the full sun.

She had lost years of a broken heart.

Loud cries emerged from deep.

In her soul was strapped a dad,

Who was never in the driver's seat.

He left his bud, and had fallen drunk,

In the barren field for thirty years.

The Pillow

I spent my life being afraid

To touch the weeds,

And pick the seeds,

From the high-rising field—

Too scared to be wounded.

I thought I would be broken

From my climb leading to the top of the stairs.

On my soft face,

I saw the mountain herb.

I could not curb,

For my fear would not cease.

I died from the continent

Of my drunken composition.

With the strength of distance,

I parted from the still steam

That shadowed the shore,

And formed my own pillow.

The Small Deed

From the bottom, my eyes rested

On a crafted nest, prodding through leaves,

That glowed from a bulge of branches.

It released me from my still bond—

The home of a bird.

I bent from my curiosity

To fetch the puny home.

A chill sliced through my head

To see the half-feathered bird staring

At my endless watered face.

Though tempted, I did not touch,

For I wanted them to last.

In the terrified gap,

I calmly retreated from their relaxed space,

For their mother to recline.

Only You

To think of you only

Is to think of a perfect you,

Which is dumb like a dead leaf.

You are a stranger

To the existence of the sphere.

Your flute needs air,

And your darkness needs light.

The rushing heart needs a chance.

The balance of nature boils down

To the hands of many.

Home from the War

Rest upon my eyes,

My heart sashayed for months

In the melting desert.

The severity of your region

Had hardened my face.

You gave all your exclusive worth,

And that is the expected stance,

For the unborn and our country.

You're no more miles away,

But in the station of my heart.

Your room there is gone,

With the miles of the old jetting sound.

Leave the war upon the shore today.

Leave the theories, and the films,

And the noise that bellows

From competition of man to man.

The Ground

Summer long brought finely dew

That came unexpectedly.

It was more welcomed than the long oak tree

That grew in the dark,

And stood coldly like ice in white.

A heart just could not elope in its icy gears

That burned and shivered joints—

A dear joint with its steam,

And toppled faces in a war of cold.

It is not easy to swallow the heat of the ground

When blades of the sun pattern the earth,

And lay in your back like a wedge.

The Icy Months

I hope you are not alone

In the swelling of the icy white month,

Where vapor advances from fresh piles,

And the verse of wind dies.

Connect yourself with obedient hands,

If you must face this side

That serves colder water.

On your humongous refrigerator, read the prints

That echo not from the flute,

But the squared television set.

In the brightness of your room,

Keep your head warm

From the dark of the falling noon,

That obediently listens to the twinkling nature—

Your rock be it your home.

The Next Page

After the last flight,

I unfolded everything within,

And let go the imperfect bar

That lies parallel—

To the raw frame.

The smoky clouds

Wore along the soul,

To cut away the great verse

That tapered in the distance.

The Light

Light the lamp. Turn the bulb.

Don't sit in the deep drained dark.

Life is a privilege.

You don't need anything else to sail—

Just you.

Put on your waiting shoes,

And be true to the world and to you.

Don't sit in the tangled dark.

Climb the hill.

Thread the mill.

Walk the forest from east to west.

Don't linger if you don't find you.

Go from north to south.

With your gentle mouth,

Increase to the blooming peak

As you seek.

Santa

Santa came to the street

With loads of sweet-scented smiles.

Shaded in the wide arm chair,

He glared at people from miles.

His charm funneled the crowd nearby.

Filled hands opened the season

That long awaits the promise.

It seems a special reason.

Laughter burst quicker than the ocean waves,

And tears dropped and drowned on dull faces,

With the pool of love in awaking boxes

That unfurled on the waiting surfaces.

The scary banging bells of hearts reclined,

As people find this fellow

That reminded them of the infinite gift above.

Heavenward was the reminded rule of below.

The Old Track

I heard the train

That covered the heart of steel,

And whirl the arms of leaves,

With warring interlude,

In the stream of daybreak.

At windows, heads lit

Like fine seeds,

As they disappeared from the breeze,

And branched off to the mere dark.

The disoriented trees

Were what left in a second,

Of the ability not to spend time,

Where the road merged—

And where the standard of buildings set.

The Silent Water

Let us go to the river at the silent water.

The drought had gained its heart,

And the leaves have spread their wreaths.

In her bed, the summary of moaning scatters.

I know it was really frail,

Waiting on a drink from above,

Freshly for its habitat.

Go

Go enjoy the eclipse,

The burning earth,

The fresh buds upon the air,

And the swelling ocean's tides.

Don't buckle your burden! Blow out!

Make one's heart free,

And one's lips fine.

Don't go in sleep.

Go and give praise for breath

That secretly lies inside,

Watching the mountain share,

And the little insects that increased their sails.

Hands for Christmas

There are hands for Christmas,

Where the golden lights swallow the trees,

And where many hearts are free.

The world stays bright,

And many heads have their flights.

Stay from toil all year long, souls.

Many ears melt close to the sound of voices.

The cold hearts sleep,

As they come to the end of the steep.

From the white nature's songs,

The past stayed gone,

And smiles make a mark,

From the heart of a cart,

At the end of a year's heart.

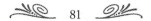

Supermarket Evening

The unrest sun pooled us on the log,

And gained our moment of energy.

Our perfect knit compressed in chattering,

Loud outbursts from our innocent lips.

It enlightened the neighborly dull air.

Our winding feet in the dust—

Destroyed the silhouette of our skin.

The barking of each car at the gate

Always steered us out of the circle,

As our eyes waited to catch the light of our mother,

Who had traveled far each busy day.

Her presence would pivot us

In counting stars, as her heart came

To our whole with a snack,

Or just a tasty pause.

Our unit would buff with glee.

This too was her golden moment.

The Corner Shop

Several miles took me to the corner shop,

Drinking sweat like the pulling sea.

Now the inside setting was scaling even more.

I suddenly lost the heat,

And became cold in my new scene.

That was the feeling of bearing the images,

Of idlers who hang out like rocks,

When I needed the ecstasy of my own heart—

The moment of not remembering salt

To prepare the daily meals.

From my scary journey of brief,

Through the none welcomed woods,

The unseen birds filled the distance of grief,

And trees form images that puffed my head

To the unreachable sky.

This time of the crawling evening sustained me.

Back to our unceasing poverty that sprouted like thorns,

That nailed this weather

And the sudden rush of the closing world,

Without sympathy for anyone.

On the Wood

The ancient stories receded,

The hard cover of the day,

As we plunged deep,

In the soul of another human,

To fill our thirsts.

Looking at granddad

As he perfectly delivered inland,

We felt like we were unveiling the husk,

As our darkest evening swept,

Sitting on the soundless wood.

Between the Dark and the Light

When the world closes its eyes,

Followed were children, cornered,

On the ground, slipping in laughter.

As their faces meet,

It lifted their nights,

Not knowing of television and its ties.

The radio they heard of

Was not a package in their habitat.

The arms of parents were too weak.

The huge yard was the inclusion,

For their own liveliness screen.

In the midst of the black,

The bonded team sprinkled love on the icy tour—

With old songs on the lips—

And the action of love from their arms,

Though sometimes hunger pitched;

And the old story of not having,

Was a forgetful hour.

The Cold Woods

Blowing the fire—made me hungrier

Than the old poor smoke

That covered my dream.

For minutes, I watched before the birth

Of the shadow of blaze.

I was furious in my survival trap.

My continual attendant to this

Rolled me back to the city light—

Of the fine atmosphere indeed.

With my water boiling against this hour,

I know I would be awake.

I will blow someday with the rules.

I am only human and it only takes growth.

The Flooded Track

With tears, she dares not to stop,

Pulling her limbs through the rubble

That was flooding with its own sentence,

Bridging nights with its political endeavor.

She was wounded and hurt,

But not a fool to heal at the bottom,

And not able to sing the song of recognition

Of her own literature.

The Red Bus

The burning flame of poverty

Was too true not to be recognized.

In the minds of those affected,

This was not jazz,

That decorated laughter.

As my academy path aroused,

The shuddering surface,

Of trailing backward to the window,

Was not easy.

The motionless days of my mom,

Battered pockets,

The crack of many things,

And the wonder of what next.

The hanging on doorsteps

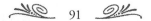

Was the dried unequal terms of the day.

The flooding of ideas and the jails of gates drove the vent.

A broken mind stirred with the conductor of the last step.

Like a buttress or an angel,

This leaflet was one of the most uneasiness,

As my stomach rode in the sand packed bus.

I was horrified and weak from the charge,

But from the black within

I fought for the years of peace.

First Day at Kindergarten

The fairy of rose enhanced,

That I would be a part of her bosom

For every single second.

The rain had washed this record.

Was it easy?

No, a nostalgic of epicenter,

And the groaning,

Occurred like eternity, measuring the going hugs.

I felt incarcerated in the hearts of the unknown,

With not much promise of changing the trials,

From not a grave scene.

The briefly performed therapy

Could not furnish the image

Of the regrettable absence of my stronghold.

I was marooned by the elements of school life.

That was what it seems.

I learned it late, and forgave myself on that day.

My teachers were not trying to butcher me,

But giving me a lifetime opportunity.

My mother had the ability to run alone,

Without me at every meet.

Sad mom, for that was the avenue to be grown.

You let go of my hand,

And I formed the other part.

My Neighbor

Just after six, the noise swept through our backyard.

Children screamed like the weeping willow,

When heads should find comfort like a pillow.

My breakfast was torn apart

Beneath the fading lamplight.

This was nothing I wanted to consume.

Something could spill an unhappy journey

For the running days ahead.

In the clinging cry, I felt as heavy as lead.

My dad and I went out to investigate the accused voices.

Instead, we were drowned in tears,

For little Polly's burned hands.

"Poor child," dad said,

Watching her mom's dying face,

Fading in the new day traced.

I think dad was more relieved than I.

"I am so sorry," he said.

I know he was happier,

For it was better than dying.

That was what I concurred,

Polly can live again.

It measured in the thought of two.

The Entrance of the Storm

Who knows the entrance of the storm?

When will the wind hit,

Or the noise will scare?

The dancing trees may fall.

The saving fruits may say goodbye.

The baked soil may silt, run, and partner with the valley,

Which will deepen our cry,

If the ditch becomes our drowning path.

Who knows, for it is now.

We have to go through our war,

Break away the rocks that were once cemented,

Destroy the boom that will explode,

And wake the souls that sleep.

It is time to remain stronger than the growth,

Of the running weeds that are not needed—

Not for the journey ahead.

The Heavy Sun

I saw you burning in the heavy sun.

It patterned your face in stone-like strips,

As you war to keep the light

And the vibration going.

The vanishing field of new pierced your skin.

As your crops bled this drop, reddened eyes appeared.

In the cold day you knew your call.

You had to convert the lonesome acres

From the shadow of more roaring scars.

This was like breathing in a skeleton.

The tying wound was great,

But you were greater than the fall.

This cemetery only needed the living.

Mile Post to Mile Post

The reality of bared feet,

And a few small books, steered us

Into much of a sport icon—

Clocking with the clock,

Running from pole to pole,

In the swelling afternoon sun,

Resting a little with burning thirst,

For our bags were not formed with bottles.

Many got relief with a sugar liquid at noon,

The signified lunchtime for the scholars—

That died with the break hours,

Before our feet turned for home.

I wonder, maybe this was what caused our energy

On the unending asphalt that steered us homeward.

On arrival, we knew dinner sometimes never awake,

Due to the lack of firewood or personnel to get the grocery.

Luckily, it was not from far-fetched.

Many times I preferred tearing down the high-blade grass,

Hoping to pound upon a yellow gut guava tree.

My stomach would not have to war,

But the long awaiting dinner would be just a blessing.

Thankful Nature

The loss of my dog held me hostage under the pear tree.

A perfect animal, I noted as I grew frantic.

In the full sun this great version of love

Would meet me at our gate,

Hanging unto me like a flower bud,

With flashing tail of excitement,

As he wedded me in his heart.

My heart now burned,

For this young heart that tore my rising dream.

Yet I never know—

I was truly glad for the barren pear tree

That let me understand.

He had saved me from much blackness.

In my runs,

Heroes died too—

After they have taught you how to live.

Mango Season

It was after the sweat rolled off our faces from play,

We would drown ourselves in the heavy journey.

Long crocus bags we borrowed from the aching kitchen butchery,

Were sweetly folded in the belly of our hands.

That always seemed to be ill,

But grandpa always promised it would be fine.

I guess it was now tired.

The shaky outlook was from its failed years.

The vision of reaching the river banks

Was not weakened by crowded grass coldly laid,

And tame bugs pierced and hugged our skins,

Our strong energies and molded faces exercised more caution.

As we gained closer sight, our eyes pointed in the direction

Of the swirling trees and the winding river.

Mangoes were decked softly on the long cold shore.

Many won our hearts, and some anchored in tears.

Often times our arms were still.

The mourning of abundant sound,

Expelled from the distressed of the whining voyage.

Our noses were packed with the seriousness of mixed pungent,

And we warned each not to climb,

For the river bank needed more arms

Than what we could offer.

We could only stand to the test,

Though we breathed a little higher.

Who doesn't like much fresher blooms?

The Awaken Hands

It was not so of autumn,

Constantly tearing down the leaves

Of the only shade in the small space,

And pooling them up

In the wide awakening morning,

And in the disgruntled sun in the afternoon.

But it was my aching mom,

In the height of the peanut crops,

With the blades that noisily echoed

And pinched her skin.

It was less of inhumane alone,

Watching my mom fighting the earth

To heal our hearts.

It kicked me several nights,

And I slept in tears.

Many nights, the same bags would remain,

Without her seeing a market to sell her toil.

This was more of a depression

In the folded blurred room,

As bats and flies injured our sights

From the sleeping bags that would not leave this deck.

Mom continued, though I thought she was stripped

From her spring of happiness.

Early morning wake became a routine.

She would plant the same nuts

That seemed to take a decade to go.

At the Gate

I could not fathom, no not the visitor,

That came to the house—

My mathematics teacher had perfect timing.

I cried as I shivered in the hiding place

In the depth of my room.

Mathematics was not my dream—

Adding and checking was great,

But in the ice of high school

The new terms ran too fast,

And I could not rise fast enough to retain.

No matter how the professor preached the rules.

I suffered greatly for losing out,

And now he was making it worse.

Maybe relating my crippling scores—

It could only ache from inside.

The burning ache, widening, faced my mother.

As she came closer she seemed full size,

And I wondered how she seemed so cool—

She was, and my color changed.

So overwhelmed, she shared my teacher's interest

In giving extra classes, and I wondered if I could make her
    happier.

The Moon Between

Two shadows lurking in the sand,

And fresh breeze covered our hands.

Widely apart we perched,

As the night shadowed in.

We knew we had to pack up our thoughts,

And fly like the breeze to our homes;

For the wall would come caving in,

As much as we want to change,

And beg for the sun.

The moon on the hill signified,

The curtain would soon be closed;

And we breathed heavily with our ticket,

Through waiting to have another night out,

Just close to him—yet a mile in the distance.

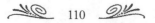

Couldn't Wait

By the crackling of a hen,

I knew there was the descendant of an egg.

At the entrance, many times I could not figure—

Not for the bird

That had long birth,

And staging its deliverance.

I would chase its path,

Pushing down heavy grasses

That seemed like they never knew

When to stop growing.

As they intruded in my journey,

Making the well-known field the ache of my heart,

The village grass pushed me backward,

But I knew in her privacy lay an egg

That needed to come to the shore of my hands.

Champion above the Water

Are you a champion?

Does this ever flash across your face?

You need to know what you settle for,

And whether it is enough;

When the compass lives,

And when you moan of death in its set.

You must know if you give too much,

Or if you give too little.

You must know the seed you sow,

And the care you show.

And whether it was enough—

During the test and the rough.

You must know how many times

You're to be blamed for not being right,

And the many reasons to give up before the start.

And why the sanction of failing art.

You must know the effect of a calm hill,

Or a hill that echoes noise.

A living champion knows the naked truth

Of living verses and dying.

Country Route

Come eat—

My grandma has enough

On her heavy trees:

Apple red, guava with a thousand seeds,

Yellow bananas, and cherries that don't fall.

She gives all,

For you are her children.

Though not of birth, you're hers from the farther sun.

The village belongs to her,

Come mix—you are all hers.

These trees are waiting to sing songs with you

While you feast on fruits.

Whole in the Wind

Deep in the bosom she slept whole—tears were gone.

Now mom could turn another page,

Watching the little light

Dancing in her sight.

As the scaling fever blast away,

From so near the carcass of the wind—now was gone.

Mom laughed from the scared,

Formalizing the clear.

Nothing now could intoxicate her.

She was whole,

And there was no reason standing in a hole.

My Uncle Never Lost

My uncle never lost,

Not even when the extraordinary grass

Was abusing his crops.

He would laugh big and strong,

Then utter, "There goes another lingering test,

And I must not lose.

I must find the key to this."

His face would start to think.

He would not talk much, not about the failure that lurked,

But his strength, as his eyes wore the grass.

He framed his plants lively underneath the sky,

With his head high, and looked the look of success

As he marries the newly image.

Shape

Shape your world in the way you care,

And when the battle of wars is at your door,

You already know what you want.

For years ago you had never drowned.

You have grown,

And you just have to show now,

Just what you have learned.

Shouting in the Sand

The flowers of our hearts

Bloom in hard sand,

And take lost soul from aching depth of the sea

To a milder cleave of arms.

The flowers of our hearts break the pain

In the distance that glared,

And lower the shooting mountains

That break the hurdles we must pass.

Unwrapping the Poverty

Let us break the poverty;

It can be done.

Enough is enough—

Let us march to the city light,

And let the dark moan.

Let our ribs be strong—

Our fears diminish from the dust,

And our mood brightens

Like the irresistible sun.

Let us forget the tears

And stand on our ground—

The payable ground with no wrong.

The War on the Ground

Men with hoes and machetes,

And washers of hard to bear clothes,

Were the brothers and sisters we shared.

These completed the aliveness and root of the day.

At the grocery shops, customers called serve

For the rice and sugar that ran out.

We watched the fat bananas—

Yellow and green on the counters—

Settled without complaining about the staring eyes.

Salt mackerel and herring shouted loudly

In their April pails,

And you had to hold your stomach

As your dream runs out.

That was not what you were about,

And you could only set your feet back;

On the asphalt that burned like pepper,

Singing children's songs till you meet your mile.

With your goods and change you smile,

Then go running to doll's house,

Where you dramatized the doctor or the nurse.

It felt good, and you only wanted then to dream higher.

The ragged clothes we knew we could change,

And take leave of absence from the fields.

The Ugly Fight

There was a lot to live for in the day,

Yet it grew hard;

Strange enough we all had to arrange our hearts,

For the best in the worst.

Watching our own suffer

From the unflinching pain,

Kicked us all around the globe,

As our dreams could not rise at our gate.

Many times in the closing nights,

We were on our knees, not single,

As the air swarmed with grief.

We buried our play for the fighting of this dream,

And our right to live with him.

That was the road for us as children.

Bush Fire

The angry fire was close to the border

Of granddad's farm.

It was winding way to the center with intense heat.

Grandpa's strongest thought was to discourage

Before it rearranged his heart,

As the steaming bright blood echoes,

Covering a perfect day like snow,

And leaving the ravages of its play.

Nature permits the river close,

And granddad's scream

Raised the city at his toes.

The prescription was to remedy,

Its fighting power to go viral in its time.

The mayhem of sorrow loads

From the unsettled heat that gushed

The heads of uncounted men,

And nature ended the tears.

Catapult

Boys with catapult vacated their birth home

With the head of just a taste of a bird.

In the full breeze,

Handcuffing and releasing randomly,

Brutal thorns that abused.

They would leave them bleeding among the grass,

As they turned their backs;

To high grown trees,

To restore their love for the catching of birds.

With a catapult and a stone.

A Bundle of Wood

He dragged the bundle of wood

To the ground,

Sending chickens flying.

In his golden moment, he released,

From his hectic distant of ax fighting,

And non-caring bugs

That knifed his skinny flesh,

In the milky land of fresh trees.

Their dull moments initiated the sweat,

And the stopping moment.

Yet as soon as this fiesta vanished,

The afternoon led back to his home.

In the Distance

The long, winding road

Led to the sawing of woods,

And loud machine that took

Away the country's horns,

And the inspiration from a man two decades older.

The draining sun,

That ceased his feet a dozen times,

Wrapped him under the running branch

That shades the unending banks,

As he looked back at home.

He needs to be present, and he could not be impetus,

For his mom was just extending her care;

And only he could fail her,

For she was matching him in his era.

The New Baby

The perturbing stomach was downsized,

And the winding in of a new birth was fulling.

It was not from my mother,

But her wonderfully made sister,

And the enriching eyes from this little angel.

It was wrapping my sleep up,

As I study the details of forming her in my space.

My thoughts spiked, my heart leaped,

And I was contented—waiting on her

To cling in our native land.

The Wire that Part

How strong was the wire

That separated our neighbor's dream from ours?

We still meet—not at the gate

But at the wire—

Laughing and bubbling in the old fire.

What did the wire part us from?

Is the snake never seen?

Or the cautious rules that embedded?

The Village Price

Bottles line up without a count.

They took a major section of the hollow room,

Like they were nicely fixed furniture.

Yet they served the domestic session

That grew from purposes.

The pain in the wind rose at its low.

Often the shout,

And steam in the regression,

Of the challenging moments of not in stock.

Splashing was not read on the surfaces of floor.

Holding zinc and board for heavy breathing,

Waiting in lines was not a great session.

That moment the piling of heavy towels rode,

And tired heads bawled.

Exercises of hands were done with force,

As the long distance measures faith.